Ancient
ROMAN ART

Susie Hodge

Heinemann LIBRARY

D0271219

First published in Great Britain by Heinemann Library
Halley Court, Jordan Hill, Oxford OX2 8EJ
a division of Reed Educational and Professional Publishing Ltd

OXFORD FLORENCE PRAGUE MADRID ATHENS
MELBOURNE AUCKLAND KUALA LUMPUR SINGAPORE TOKYO
IBADAN NAIROBI KAMPALA JOHANNESBURG GABORONE
PORTSMOUTH NH CHICAGO MEXICO CITY SAO PAULO

Produced by Plum Creative
Illustrations by Oxford Illustrators
Printed in Hong Kong / China

500 587550

01 00 99
10 9 8 7 6 5 4 3 2

ISBN 0 431 05628 5 (HB) ISBN 0 431 05607 2 (PB)

British Library Cataloguing in Publication Data
Hodge, Susie
    Ancient Roman art. – (Art in history)
    1. Art, Roman – Juvenile literature
    I. Title
    709.3'7

Acknowledgements
The Publishers would like to thank the following for permission to reproduce photographs:
AKG photo, E.Lessing pp.11 (right), 13, 28, Vatican Museums p.4; Ancient Art & Architecture Collection Ltd, R.Sheridan p.10 (left); The Bridgeman Art Library, pp.14–15, Giraudon p.19, Metropolitan Museum of Art, New York p.7, Museo Archaeologico Nazionale, Naples pp.6, 11 (left), Museo & Gallerie Nazionali di Capodimonte, Naples p.10 (right), Museum of Antiquities, Newcastle upon Tyne p.9; Corbis, R.Ergenbright p.25, R.Nowitz p.27, R.Vanni p.26, A Woolfitt p.20; C.M.Dixon pp17, 18, 24; Giraudon pp.22–23, Lauros pp.5, 12, 21, Mermet p.8; Michael Holford p.29

Cover photograph reproduced with permission of Bridgeman Art Library.

Our thanks to Paul Flux and Jane Shuter for their comments in the preparation of this book.

Every effort to contact copyright holders of any material reproduced in this book. Any omissions will be rectified in subsequent printings if notice is given to the Publisher.

*Cover picture: Wall painting from the Villa of Mysteries, Pompeii, mid 1st century BC, height 1.5 m, **fresco**.*
Roman people who could afford to, paid artists to paint the walls in their homes. During the 1st century BC, a style of wall painting developed that became known as the Second Style. Artists painted pictures that were so lifelike they looked real. In this villa just outside Pompeii, the mistress of the house asked the artist to paint a Roman story of a religion that we no longer know anything about. So the paintings have given the villa its name, the Villa of Mysteries. The artist has painted life-size, lifelike people against a brilliant red background. This is one of the most well-known examples of this style of painting, famous because of the outstanding skill of the artist.

CONTENTS

WHAT WAS ROMAN ART?

Near the River Tiber in Italy, several small villages on seven hills grew to become the city of Rome. By 509BC Rome was a **republic**. Gradually its power grew until it became a vast **empire**. By AD100, Rome ruled over most of the then known world.

Adopting traditions

The Romans took over many countries, including Carthage (in North Africa), Gaul (which stretched from Italy to the Netherlands), Greece, Egypt and Britain. They adopted the traditions that appealed to them, such as the countries' religion or art. Romans ruled, organized and taxed the people of these countries, often mixing the best of Rome with the best of other cultures.

Many people from Rome's captive countries were employed by the Romans. Greek and Egyptian artists, for example, used their own methods to produce art for the Romans.

*Augustus, Prima Porta near Rome, about 19BC, 2.04 m, **marble**.*

*This statue of the first Roman emperor Augustus (31BC–AD14) is by a Greek sculptor. The Romans admired the dignity of Greek **portraits** in statue form. They wanted their emperor shown as a commanding, godlike person. The back of this statue was unfinished because Roman statues stood against walls.*

Lifelike details

So the Romans took on other traditions, but added their own likes and dislikes. They admired the beauty and perfection of Greek art but they preferred lifelike details that showed people's oddities and character.

Powerful achievements

The Romans employed artists and workmen throughout their empire to produce impressive art and to build great roads and buildings. Art and **architecture** were used to honour the gods, to celebrate events or to proclaim someone's power. They were not just for decoration, although that was important, too. It is a sign of Roman power that their style remained similar in different lands. The Romans have had an enormous influence on art and architecture ever since.

The Triumphal Arch Of Tiberius, southern France, about AD30, height 18.3 m, stone.

Arches to proclaim victories were set up all over the Roman Empire. These and other buildings were designed with different sized arches and columns to make them more interesting to look at.

MATERIALS AND METHODS

Who became an artist?

Architects (master builders and designers), were usually educated people of the middle class. They created some of the grandest monuments in the history of **architecture**. Other artists (all called craftsmen) were usually poorer **citizens**. They worked in small workshops with a few **apprentices** and one or two slaves. Many Greek artists set up workshops so Roman artists could learn from them. Most paintings or statues were commissioned, or ordered, by wealthy citizens. Artists rarely signed their work because they were only doing a job. Artists were not thought to be special.

*Bust of Emperor Vespasian, about AD75, **marble**.*

*A bust is a statue of the head and shoulders. Roman artists made a **portrait** of anyone who could afford to pay them. They did not try to make portraits perfect, but enjoyed showing a person's characteristics. Even though he was the emperor, this bust shows Vespasian's wrinkled skin, large nose and serious expression. Statues of emperors were put up all over the **empire** as a reminder that the Romans were in control.*

What materials did they work with?

Brushes were made from twigs, wood, lengths of reeds or rushes. They were sometimes bound with hair. Shaped wood and ivory sticks were used for drawing and writing. They were called styluses. Many wall paintings were made of paint mixed with egg yolk, called tempera. Some were in encaustic, in which colours are mixed with wax and burned into the surface with hot irons. But most were painted in **fresco**.

For tempera and encaustic, the walls had to be smooth. They were prepared with a coating of cement, **plaster** and marble dust, which was polished before it was painted. For frescoes, walls were coated with plaster. The paint was then applied while the plaster was still wet. Most statues were polished and then painted in tempera.

Garden of Livia, Prima Porta near Rome, about 50–40BC, height 1.52 m, fresco.

This is one of many wall paintings discovered in a Roman house. It is filled with fruit trees, flowers and birds. Bluish colours help to show distance and space, brighter colours seem close-up and shadows make some objects look solid.

SIGNS AND SYMBOLS

Many of our words and alphabet letters come from Latin, which was the common language of the Roman **Empire**. Having one common language meant that people from different countries could communicate with each other.

Most Roman **citizens** were encouraged to learn to read. In large cities like Rome and Alexandria there were many bookshops, libraries and publishers.

How books were made

Books were usually **scrolls** made out of papyrus, an Egyptian reed. The reed was cut into long narrow strips; soaked and pressed together; beaten with a mallet; left to dry; and finally polished smooth with a stone.

Each book had to be written out by hand. Someone read the book to several scribes who copied the book down. Each scribe made a copy on the papyrus using reed pens. The Latin words were written in columns. Some of the scribes were artists, too, and many books were beautifully illustrated.

Virgil and the Muses, end of 2nd century to early 3rd century AD, **mosaic**.

This mosaic shows the famous poet Virgil sitting between two muses. Muses are goddesses who inspire writers and artists. Virgil holds a papyrus scroll of his greatest poem, The Aeneid.

Roman letters

Scribes and stonemasons painted or carved inscriptions (words) on their monuments and statues. Two main kinds of letters were used: square capital letters for formal inscriptions and sloping italic letters for informal writing such as letter-writing. Each letter was made of a geometric shape such as a square, triangle or circle. At first letters in stone were carved to one thickness. Later the sides were made to vary from thick to thin. This gave the same effect as the square-tipped brushes which stonemasons used to paint the letters on the stone first.

Inscription from Milecastle, on Hadrian's Wall, Britain, AD 122–125, stone.

A castle was built every mile along Hadrian's Wall. This inscription records the building of one Milecastle by the Second Legion Augusta. The letters were chiselled by hand and the little tick-shaped marks at the ends of letters are where stonemasons rested their chisels as they carved. We use tick-shapes even now on some printed letters and call them serifs.

9

PAINTING TECHNIQUES

The Romans loved to have paintings in their homes and public buildings. They did not have wallpaper, so artists painted pictures directly on to the walls and ceilings. Floors were also painted. Small panel paintings on wood were hung on walls or displayed on **easels**. These were sold from artists' workshops.

Fresco was used for most walls. This made the colours brighter and helped the painting to last. When the background was dry, details were added. All kinds of scenes were painted, such as gods and heroes, hunting and farming, landscapes and animals. **Portraits** of the owners of houses were popular, too.

Trick pictures

Four different styles of Roman wall painting developed.

First style Walls were painted to look as if they were made of **marble**, or were copies of Greek styles of decoration.

House of Citharist, Stabiae, Naples, 1st century BC, fresco.

This house had a series of frescoes running around it that were similar to Greek homes. Some houses had marbled effects painted on the walls.

Second style Realistic looking scenes tricked the eye. They looked like views through windows.

Room from the Villa of Mysteries, Pompeii, mid 1st century BC, height 1.5 m, fresco.

The background of brilliant red and the black dividing lines do not look realistic, but the life-sized figures certainly do. 29 figures and numerous scenes run continuously round the room, making it appear larger than it really is.

Third style Less realistic, but often delicate looking pictures.

Spring, Maiden Gathering Flowers, Stabiae, Naples, about 15BC–AD60, fresco.

This might be a goddess or simply the lady of the house picking flowers as if in a dance. Gracefully draped in a coloured robe, this is painted in a gentle, fresh style.

Fourth style A combination of the second and third styles.

Healing of the Wounded Aeneas by Iapyx, Pompeii, 1st century AD, fresco.

This painting shows the story of doctor Iapyx healing the hero Aeneas. The goddess Venus heals him too, although the humans cannot see her.

Paint palette

Paints were made from ground rocks, powdered plants or animal dyes. Red and yellow came from ochre (a clay-like substance); white came from chalk; green from green earth; blue from a mixture of glass and copper; black from soot; and purple from a special seashell. The **pigments** were mixed with lime, milk, egg or **gum** to make a paste.

11

STORY-TELLING PICTURES

As well as inscriptions and books, the Romans used paintings and **reliefs** to tell stories of their war victories. The Greeks had done this, too. But where the Greeks used **symbolism** to tell their stories, the Romans showed the real, sometimes gory, details.

Ancient customs

These narrative, or story-telling, pictures had been a custom hundreds of years before in China. During those times, kings ordered monuments announcing their victories in war. Later these monuments developed into complete picture-stories. Wealthy Romans liked the idea of proclaiming Roman triumphs for all to see. Artists were employed to paint or carve heroic stories.

*Trajan's Column, Rome, AD 113, height of column 38 m, **marble**.*

The emperor Trajan ordered a huge column to be made to show the story of his wars. As in a comic strip, Trajan appears in a continuous, lively story that spirals around the column.

12

*The Great Hunt, Piazza Armerina, Sicily, early 4th century AD, **mosaic**.*

Artists from Africa made this large floor mosaic. The most important part of the picture is the figures. Their hair and clothes, and the animals' fur and feathers are detailed, although the trees and rocks are small and decorative. Trying to make the picture look realistic was not the aim. The picture was to tell a story and look attractive.

Art for everyone

Like advertising today, these great works of art convinced and persuaded people. They proudly announced victories. At the same time, they told people that the Roman **Empire** was the greatest.

Most narrative art was about battles. Some stories of gods, goddesses, heroes and legends were also painted and carved. Roman art was meant to be seen and enjoyed by many. Artists worked hard at making it easily understood.

Public and private art

Works of art that showed the Roman Empire and its emperors as strong and generous were put in public places for all to see. Story-telling pictures were painted inside private houses – these were done by interior decorators, not major artists.

13

MOSAIC ART

Mosaics became popular from the 1st century AD. They were pictures or patterns made from small pieces of coloured glass or stone. They decorated walls and floors.

How mosaics were made

Artists drew a design of the mosaic they were going to make. Then they spread wet **plaster** over a small area of the floor or wall and smoothed it down. They quickly pressed the pieces of stone into the plaster while it was still damp, following their design.

At first, patterns in black and white were the most common. They remained fashionable around Rome. But further afield, by the 2nd century AD, more colourful mosaics became popular. Companies of artists designed mosaics in their workshops. People chose a design, then the mosaic artist came to the house with the chosen plan and the stones already cut. Several artists would work on one mosaic.

Orpheus Playing to the Animals, Antioch in Turkey, about 2nd century AD, mosaic.

The Roman god, Orpheus, plays a lyre, charming the animals around him. Shadows and highlights make the picture look three-dimensional. See how contented all the animals look as they listen to the music!

Make your own mosaic

Materials:

several sheets of coloured paper or card
scissors
glue
large sheets of white paper or card
pencil

1 Cut the coloured paper or card into small squares.

2 Draw the outline of your mosaic on a large sheet of white paper or card.

3 Stick the coloured squares in place on your outline, leaving a tiny space between each of your squares, so that the mosaic looks realistic.

Bird and Bunch of Grapes, Badajoz in Spain, about 350BC, mosaic.

Brightly coloured pieces of stone called tesserae have turned this wall into a beautifully decorated area. It is meant to be more of a pattern than realistic, although you can see clearly what it represents. Mosaics in this style were used to decorate fountains too.

15

ART FOR THE GODS

The Romans adopted religions as well as styles of art from the countries they took over. They gave their adopted gods and goddesses different names. For example, Aphrodite was the Greek goddess of love and beauty. The Romans called her Venus. Until Christianity was adopted, the Romans did not believe in worshipping just one god. Because of this, it made sense to allow the people in the country they took over to keep their old gods.

The Romans did not believe that their art showed real events. They were made to remind people about the gods they were worshipping and to please the gods themselves. Some pictures showed people performing rituals for the gods. Some showed wondrous stories of supernatural strength and power. Some, like the figures on the breastplate of Augustus on page 4, showed that the gods protected the good and the great.

Mars and Venus, from the House of Lucrezio Frontone, Pompeii, 1st century AD **fresco**.

According to Roman religion, Mars, the god of war, loved Venus. Roman artists often painted the two together, sometimes showing them as ordinary humans. Mars stands behind wearing military dress, with helmet. Venus, sitting in front of him, wears a long tunic and light cloak, like a wealthy Roman woman. Cupid, the god of love, stands in the centre, whilst other citizens look on.

Household gods

The Romans worshipped thousands of gods and spirits. The most important gods and goddesses were Jupiter, Neptune, Venus and Minerva. They were well known to Roman **citizens** throughout the **empire** because all kinds of art had been made in the gods' honour. Apart from the main gods, every house had its own shrine called a Lararium. At this shrine the people worshipped the household gods, called Lares, every day. The Lararium was often carved and decorated, with small statuettes and painted friezes (decorations that run in a band).

Venus Marina, Pompeii, before AD79, fresco.

Venus, the goddess of love, is in a magical seashell, being towed by Cupid and some dolphins. She did not have to look realistic because she is a symbol. The artist has made her up from his imagination. This fresco and many others were painted on the walls of houses in Pompeii and Herculaneum. The walls were covered in volcanic ash when the volcano Vesuvius erupted in AD79. This preserved the frescoes.

17

ROMAN SCULPTURE

Sculptors and stonemasons were hired to make statues for public buildings and private villas. Statues were brightly painted, but the paint has now worn off. Gods, goddesses, animals and **portraits** of real people were common subjects.

*Titus, Rome, about AD80, height 1.96 m, **marble**.*

*This portrait of the Emperor Titus was part of a full-length sculpture that showed him commanding everyone to look up to him by looking stern and mighty. It was made to show his power and importance. Statues of emperors were put up all over the **empire** as a reminder that the Romans were in control.*

Commemorative statues

There was great demand for **commemorative** statues. They were placed in public squares, halls or temples. Some were put on top of commemorative columns. Most were of emperors and other important people, symbolizing victory and power. Sculptors had learned from Greek sculptors how to show draped material over what appears to be a living body. They enjoyed the challenge of creating realistic looking fabric hanging in folds on the body, as well as realistic looking faces. Along with statues in armour, these portrait statues were grand and lifelike reminders of their rulers to the **citizens** of the Roman Empire.

Scenes from everyday life

Roman artists also carved details from daily life. Often these were made for sarcophagi (stone coffins) or tombstones to tell stories of a dead person's life. These **relief** carvings show scenes like mothers bathing their babies, people working or relaxing or wedding ceremonies. They all seem natural looking and relaxed. They also give us a wonderful insight into everyday Roman life.

Roman butcher, 2nd century BC, stone frieze.

This relief probably decorated a Roman butcher's shop. The butcher is chopping meat on a block. You can see other kinds of meat hanging on hooks above. Notice the little details that the artist has included, such as the pulley and rope and the folds of the butcher's toga.

19

CLASSICAL STYLE

The term 'classical art' usually refers to the art of the ancient Greeks and Romans. The classical style is carefully designed and balanced.

Borrowing ideas

The Romans copied the Greeks, but the Greeks originally learnt from the Egyptians. They borrowed Egyptian ideas but were able to improve such crafts as **marble** carving and **bronze casting** because they had better tools. This allowed them to create more realistic images than the Egyptians. The Romans then borrowed and adapted the Greeks' ideas.

Marcus Aurelius, AD161–80, height 3.5 m, bronze.

This is the only large-scale Roman bronze statue which has survived to the present day. After the Romans converted to Christianity, bronze statues of non-Christian emperors or gods were melted down. This statue was mistakenly believed to be of a Christian emperor, so it was not destroyed. Notice the emperor's striking pose and the lifelike horse. The whole weight of the rider and horse is carried on three thin legs. This was a difficult effect to produce.

Detailed descriptions

In the 1st century AD, a scribe called Pliny wrote an encyclopedia of natural sciences and arts. He described many Roman artists and their methods, such as the casting of bronze. Pliny's book was useful to artists centuries later. They learned skills that might otherwise have been forgotten.

Skilful sculptors

Sculptors became highly skilled, drawing many sketches, then making clay, wax or **plaster** maquettes (small test models of the sculpture). **Marble**, bronze, wood and wax were used for most statues and **reliefs**. The lost-wax method of casting was used often. First a model was made in wax. Then a clay mould was made around it. When baked, the wax melted away and the clay became the mould for the bronze to be poured into. The clay mould was later broken open to reveal the solid bronze statue.

The Goddess Hecate, Yugoslavia, about 1st century AD, marble.

The Romans loved art and colour. Most statues were brightly painted originally, but the colour has now worn away. Sculptors produced many beautifully draped female forms like this. They concentrated on proportion and balance, and made every feature stand out clearly.

SCULPTURE FOR ALL

At first it was customary to carry wax images of ancestors in Roman funeral processions. Romans believed that this preserved the dead person's soul. Later, when the **empire** stretched to distant lands, Romans burned incense in front of **busts** of their emperors, treating them like gods. Sacrifices were also brought to shrines for their gods. This proved the people's faith and devotion.

Statues everywhere

Romans put sculpture on display everywhere. Many sculptures were **portraits**. Others, like Trajan's Column on page 12, were **reliefs** that told a story, often one of Roman triumph. All these sculptures were a form of reporting and **propaganda**. They reminded people of the power of the Roman Empire.

Most sculptures were more than just decoration. Sea creatures, like dolphins which symbolized the god Cupid, were built into fountains. Gods, goddesses, heroes and animals appeared in town squares (called forums), temples, public buildings and houses. Often forums displayed statues of the town's patron god.

*Claudius, AD51–54, life-size, **marble**.*

When new, this sculpture would have been full length, brightly painted and polished. Roman sculptors produced lifelike statues of their emperors. Many later emperors thought of themselves as gods. They told their people that they should be worshipped as gods. Whether or not people really believed they were gods, it was safer to act as if they did!

22

Families

The family was important to the Romans. Statues and paintings of family members, alive and dead, were made and displayed in their homes and gardens. Statues of the Lares, gods of the household, were also shown.

Detail from The Ara Pacis Augustae, 19–13BC, height 1.6 m, marble relief.

The Ara Pacis Augustae was a large marble altar given by Emperor Augustus. It was dedicated to peace and to the people. Reliefs of stories, and patterns, are carved in detail on the walls. The stories are a mix of truth and legend. It shows Augustus, his wife, children, grandchildren (who were future emperors) and the chief priest. Notice how the people in the background are carved faintly, while those in the foreground are clearer.

ROMAN BUILDINGS

Early Roman towns had no particular plan. But as the **empire** grew and became more organized, the Romans began to arrange their towns. They needed public baths, meeting places, government buildings and temples for worship. A style for towns was developed. The most important public buildings were placed around a central forum. The rest of the town spread out from the forum in a grid pattern.

Columns and arches

The Romans used five types of column for important buildings. They are adapted from Greek columns. Roman architects and engineers also worked out how to build **domes**, **vaults** and arches.

Arches span wider gaps and support more weight than the straight beams of wood or stone that had been used previously. So, with arches, Roman buildings grew larger and stronger.

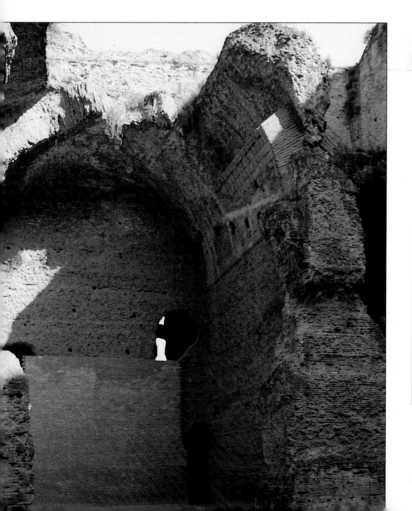

The Baths of Caracalla, Rome, AD212, originally stone, glass, concrete and **marble**.

There were public baths throughout the Roman Empire, but the ones in Rome were particularly magnificently decorated. It is hard to imagine now, but in Roman times, this ruin was a richly decorated and popular building (big enough for 1600 people). There were hot, warm and cold baths, as well as exercise and lecture rooms, libraries and snack bars. You can still see the remains of the vaulted ceilings. Vaulted ceilings were arches overlapping at right angles.

A strong invention

The Greeks had used stone for building but the Romans developed concrete. They made it with lime, sand and water, plus small stones, pieces of rock or pottery. Because concrete could be spread smoothly before drying, architects were able to develop new curved shapes on wooden frames.

By the 2nd century BC, Roman builders added powdered volcanic stone (called pumice) to make a concrete that was strong and waterproof. Architects coated the outside of concrete buildings with polished brick or marble.

The Pont du Gard, Agrippa, France, 19BC, height 49.4 m, stone.

This is another great achievement in Roman building. It is an aqueduct. It was 40 km long and built to channel water to the town of Nîmes in France. Three tiers of arches cross the River Gard. Many similar aqueducts were built throughout the empire to bring fresh water to towns.

25

BIG BUILDINGS

New building methods meant that Roman buildings and monuments were strong. Roman architects were the first to build high-rise apartment blocks!

The Pantheon, Rome, built in AD 125, replacing a smaller temple from 27BC, concrete, brick and **marble**.

This new form of temple was originally planned by Emperor Augustus's lieutenant, Agrippa. It was eventually completed when Hadrian was emperor. It is a masterpiece of both art and engineering. The domed ceiling is surprisingly large. It is 43 metres across. It was meant to represent the curved canopy of heaven. In the centre a hole, 8.5 metres across, provides light and air.

Tools and equipment

The Romans developed ways of mass producing bricks in standard sizes and shapes. Triangular-shaped bricks were baked in **kilns** to make them last longer than ordinary sun-dried bricks. Tiles and gutters were baked from clay in a similar way. Bricks set in cement were often used in arches, **domes** and **vaults**.

Various tools, such as the groma, were used to estimate straight lines. Wooden scaffolding was used to support builders as they worked and to keep blocks of stone in place. The Romans even used wooden cranes to help lift and position heavy objects. The cranes were driven by treadmills and linked to pulleys.

Huge arena

One of the most famous Roman buildings is the huge arena in Rome known as the Colosseum. Arches, vaults and concrete meant that architects could design and build this spectacular sight. It was covered in gleaming white marble, with statues in every arch.

The Colosseum was used for shows that featured gladiators or animals fighting, or the execution of enemies of the **empire**. During the interval, spectators were sprinkled with perfume to mask the smell of blood from the arena.

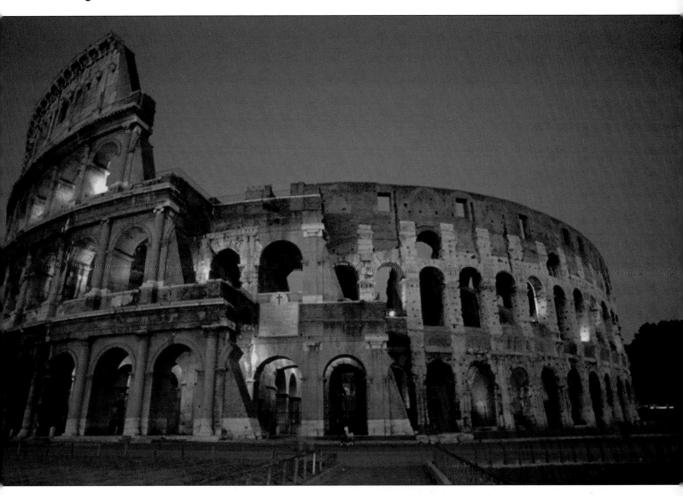

The Colosseum, Rome, AD 72–80, height 48.5 m, stone and concrete.

The Colosseum seated 50,000 spectators. Beneath the ground, a vast network of chambers housed the animals and people before their performance. The arena could even be flooded for mock naval battles. The foundations were 12 metres deep. Columns were added all around the **auditorium**. Research suggests that there could have been a movable canopy which covered the open area to shade it from the sun.

27

EARLY CHRISTIAN ART

Christians, unlike most other religious groups, worshipped only one God. This meant that they refused to worship the emperor. So at first the Romans tried to stamp out Christianity. But the number of Christians grew. In AD312 the new emperor, Constantine, became a Christian himself and made Christianity legal. Art began to change.

Secret art

For many years Christians had to worship in secret. They met in catacombs (underground passageways). They designed secret symbols and included them in paintings of Bible stories on the walls of the catacombs.

The Miracle of the Loaves and Fishes, Ravenna, Italy, about AD520, mosaic.

When Christianity was accepted, artists began using Bible stories as subjects. This shows the New Testament story when Jesus fed five thousand people with five loaves and two fish. The Romans tried to make Christianity acceptable by using familiar images from other religions. Jesus, in this picture, is copied from the old Roman god Apollo.

28

A curious mixture

We know that Roman artists could make true-to-life images, but the picture opposite looks stiff. There are shadows on the ground and in the folds of cloth, but other lifelike details were no longer necessary. It was more important to use recognizable symbols than to produce realistic art.

Church design

Christians modelled their churches on basilicas (large, rectangular assembly halls). These became the basic design for Christian churches everywhere. Statues in new churches were discouraged. But because many people could not read or write, paintings and **reliefs** taught them about their new religion.

The end of classical art

It was not just Roman art that was changing. The **empire** had grown too big and its emperors could not control it. The Roman army began to retreat from the countries around the edges of the empire. Gradually, the empire crumbled and other people took over, bringing new ideas with them.

*Symbol of Christianity, Lullingstone Villa, Kent, England, late 4th century AD, wall painting, **fresco**.*

This painting decorates a wall inside a Roman villa that was first built in the 1st century AD. It is one of the first symbols that Christians used as a mark of their beliefs. Even the colours had a special significance.

TIMELINE

BC

753	Legendary date of when Rome was founded.
509	Last king expelled from Rome, republic formed.
500	Romans begin to take over neighbouring parts of Italy.
265	Rome controls the whole of Italy.
204	Rome invades Africa.
202	Rome seizes parts of Spain.
179	First stone bridge over the River Tiber.
140	Romans conquer Greece and most of Spain.
59–51	Conquest of Gaul.
55	Invasion of Britain.
50–40	'Garden of Livia' painted. Also, wall paintings in the Villa of Mysteries, Pompeii.
30	Conquest of Egypt.
27	Augustus becomes the first emperor, (beginning of the Roman Empire).
25	Agrippa, Augustus's lieutenant and son-in-law, designs a temple in Rome.
19	The Pont du Gard aqueduct designed and built by Agrippa.
13–9	The Ara Pacis Augustae altar is built (commissioned by Emperor Augustus).
about 5	Birth of Jesus in Bethlehem.

AD

14	Tiberius becomes emperor.
79	Pliny the elder (author who described artists and their methods) dies while investigating a volcanic eruption.
30	The Triumphal Arch of Tiberius is built. Many monuments, reliefs and inscriptions are produced to tell stories of victories.
41–54	Britain is conquered. Busts and portraits of the emperors are worshipped as gods.
54–68	Emperor Nero rules and tries to get rid of all Christians.
72–80	The Colosseum is designed and built.
79–81	Titus is emperor. The volcano Vesuvius erupts (79), destroying the towns of Herculaneum and Pompeii on the west coast of Italy.
101	Trajan becomes emperor and commissions his column.
117–138	Hadrian is emperor. Builds a wall separating Britain and Scotland. The Pantheon is built on the site of Agrippa's earlier temple in Rome.
138–312	Many emperors rule. Plague, famine and wars interrupt peace and power.
312–37	Emperor Constantine rules. He becomes Christian and stops the persecution of Christians. Christian art is no longer secret art.
337–64	Many other emperors rule.
410	Roman Empire is reduced. Unrest continues.

GLOSSARY

apprentices people learning a trade or craft by working with a skilled worker

architecture the art of designing and constructing buildings

auditorium the part of a theatre where the audience (the people watching) sit or stand

bronze hard-wearing brownish gold metal. A mixture of copper and tin.

bust a sculpture of just the head and shoulders of a person

casting producing a sculpture from a mould

citizens inhabitants of a city who had many legal, political and other privileges. Not everyone was classed as a citizen – slaves, for example, were non-citizens and had no privileges.

commemorative ways of keeping things in people's memories. Memorials and celebrations are commemorative.

composition layout or arrangement of art

dome a vault rising up from a round base, usually shaped like one half of a hollow ball

easels stands or supports for holding paintings

empire land ruled by an emperor

fresco a painting made on damp, freshly plastered walls

gum sticky substance from plants, used to hold pigments together

kiln an extremely hot oven, used to bake or fire clay to harden it

marble a hard rock which can be polished to a high shine. It comes in many patterns and colours.

mosaic a picture or design made by cementing together small pieces of glass, ceramics or stone of different colours. Used on floors and walls.

pigment coloured powder made from plants, minerals or animals and mixed with various liquids to make paint

plaster a fine white powder made from a rock called gypsum. It is mixed with water, then left to dry.

portraits pictures or sculptures of a particular person or people

propaganda publicity that spreads ideas or information that will influence people

reliefs raised, carved pictures

republic a country without a hereditory ruler

scrolls books written on long sheets of paper (or papyrus) that are rolled up

symbolism pictures using symbols for meanings, rather than real, factual images

vault a curved ceiling made by arches. A barrel or tunnel vault is a group of arches together; a groin vault is two barrel vaults crossing at right angles.

INDEX

Numbers in plain type (24) refer to the text.
Numbers in bold type (**28**) refer to an illustration.